THE PORTAGE POETRY SERIES

SERIES TITLES

Catch & Release
Lauren Crawford

Steelhead
Lauren K. Carlson

The Coronation of the Ghost
Benjamin Gantcher

The Stone Tries to Understand the Hands
Susannah Sheffer

Red Camaro
Dwaine Rieves

Where Babies Come From
Ori Fienberg

Cuttings
Hannah Dow

Forgive the Animal
Sarah Pape

Love as Invasive Species
Ellen Kombiyil

They Were Horrible Cooks
Allison Whittenberg

The New Life
Wendy Wisner

Restoring Prairie
Margaret Rozga

Table with Burning Candle
Julia Paul

A Bright Wound
Sarah A. Etlinger

The Velvet Book
Rae Gouirand

Listening to Mars
Sally Ashton

Glitter City
Bonnie Jill Emanuel

The Trouble with Being a Childless Only Child
Michelle Meyer

Happy Everything
Caitlin Cowan

Dear Lo
Brady Bove

Sadness of the Apex Predator
Dion O'Reilly

Do Not Feed the Animal
Hikari Miya

The Watching Sky
Judy Brackett Crowe

Let It Be Told in a Single Breath
Russell Thorburn

The Blue Divide
Linda Nemec Foster

Lake, River, Mountain
Mark B. Hamilton

Talking Diamonds
Linda Nemec Foster

Poetic People Power
Tara Bracco (ed.)

The Green Vault Heist
David Salner

There is a Corner of Someplace Else
Camden Michael Jones

Everything Waits
Jonathan Graham

We Are Reckless
Christy Prahl

Always a Body
Molly Fuller

Bowed As If Laden With Snow
Megan Wildhood

Silent Letter
Gail Hanlon

New Wilderness
Jenifer DeBellis

Fulgurite
Catherine Kyle

The Body Is Burden and Delight
Sharon White

PRAISE FOR

Temporary Shelters

Grant Clauser writes wise and pleasing poems about "the beautiful and crumbling world." Here you'll find reflections of a life firmly grounded, planted and growing, one that celebrates tomatoes and daughters and pawpaws and brook trout and sunflowers equally, while never forgetting to mourn what is always passing from us.

—TODD DAVIS
author of *Ditch Memory: New & Selected Poems*

It's true. A great book of poems can transport you anywhere. I've had it happen to me over and again. But for a collection of poetry to bring me from the backwoods to the space station, from marshland to mountains, all the while showing me the things truly worth holding precious—the apple pies our moms make, a brook trout catching the sun just right, moonlight shining on a river's surface? That's the rarest of joys. Grant Clauser's new collection, *Temporary Shelters*, is exactly that kind of book. Line by line, these poems produce moments of pristine beauty, of snow falling "like moth wings," that simply stunt your breath. More than all that, these lines offer connection and hope (hope so pure you can taste it!) no matter what losses we face, no matter what might strafe our lives or our planet. The best gift Clauser's poems give us, though, is the reminder to breathe slowly and to "sit down in the cool morning and talk ourselves patiently into the world." For this reminder, and for this poet, I am profoundly grateful.

—JACK B. BEDELL
author of *Ghost Forest*
Poet Laureate of Louisiana, 2017-2019

In the tradition of Hopkins, Frost, and Oliver, Grant Clauser's nature poems open to the great mystery of what it means to be alive on this "slightly crooked" earth. In *Temporary Shelters* Clauser traverses the world as we know it, including "its hungry jaws," its "ruins on the one hand,/ succession on the other." And while the world "teaches us every day," about our own absences, heartaches, and hope, in Clauser's deft hands, nature also remains inimitably itself.

— ETHEL RACKIN
author of *In Time*

Temporary Shelters

poems

Grant Clauser

CORNERSTONE PRESS
UNIVERSITY OF WISCONSIN-STEVENS POINT

Cornerstone Press, Stevens Point, Wisconsin 54481
Copyright © 2025 Grant Clauser
www.uwsp.edu/cornerstone

Printed in the United States of America.

Library of Congress Control Number: 2025941723
ISBN: 978-1-960329-97-4

Cornerstone Press titles are produced in courses and internships offered by the Department of English at the University of Wisconsin–Stevens Point.

DIRECTOR & PUBLISHER
Dr. Ross K. Tangedal

EXECUTIVE EDITORS
Jeff Snowbarger, Freesia McKee

EDITORIAL DIRECTOR
Brett Hill

SENIOR EDITOR
Ellie Atkinson

PRESS STAFF
Reilly Crous, Mai Yer Lee, Brianna Loving, Josh Paulson, Sophie McPherson, Sam Bjork, Madison Schultz, Autumn Vine, Allison Lange

for Emmett and Sadie

ALSO BY GRANT CLAUSER:

POEMS

I.

II.

III.

IV.

I.

NASA Announces Plans for a Peopled Mission to Mars

I want to talk about how perfect
this brook trout is, not how fragile.
How cold and clear the creek
that ambles like a child running
her fingers over the smooth stones
of the mountain, not how it suffered
a century of coal mines and clear cutting.
Instead let's look at the rust red
stripe on a salamander's back,
its spine curving like the current
pausing around my ankles. It's true
what smart people say— every day
something beautiful is disappearing.
Every day another piece of hope
is bleached or broken or hunted
into history. I want you to know
how hard this trout fought, leaping
dams, dodging hawk and mink,
shedding parr marks for ruby spots
like wild strawberries. Today
there's light hanging from hemlock
branches, deer hair snagged on a thistle.
Consider the smell of pine needles
and rhododendron webbing the air,
how fine and fleeting it all is, how
the tendrils of fungus under the earth
bind it all together, one breathing
lumbering beast, one spectacular
world, by God, dying under our feet.

Life List

As we round the marsh, I point out
mallard, gadwall and wigeon, then confuse
merganser with loon, exhausting my taxonomy
knowledge, so instead I invent names.
There's a sharp-beaked snail sucker,
and then a duck-billed lake turkey—
probably a snow goose, but my daughter
laughs and we turn to the meadow,
where tall grasses shriek with
not-a-robins and rat-faced rat birds.
Somewhere, a buzz-saw pecker pounds
the dead wood out of a tree somehow
still standing past last spring's hardest
storms, and we keep walking into
the woods, look for the Led Zeppelin
hermit thrush we saw last year
who followed for almost a mile
strumming from tree to tree as if
trying to tell us we missed a turn
where the trail forked by the hey-hawk nest.
My field book pages slowly fill,
a story built of blending
what we know with what we don't,
stumbling into life
the way each morning happens,
young birds opening up to song,
the world made up as we go along.

Making Tomato Sauce with my Daughters During a Pandemic

So here we are, tucked into the house
with nothing but sighs to lengthen
and shorten the hours
while sickness stalks the season
like cracks in a sidewalk
children are taught to avoid.
We're listening to the kitchen radio
spill number after number,
ten more dead in our county
as we stir tomatoes in a pot,
add basil, garlic, one glug
of wine and one of olive oil,
and slowly the house turns into
something other than a house
from mixing and stirring simple things—
spaghetti pot on the stove, breadsmell from the oven,
mingle like birdcalls in the backyard
to help us forget our fear of news and neighbors,
to become a kind of blessing we savor,
acting normal when the world is not.
It's a skill, I think, not the sauce, though
that too takes practice, but the mingling
we make of this. One life kneading another.
A stolen hour becomes the heart's
temporary shelter as one day becomes the next
afternoon we soon forget. And we try to forget too
the money we've lost, the sunlight we're missing,
the ambulance pulling shadows down the road.
And how our old complaints get older
with disuse until they fade away, replaced
with new ones. And now the sauce is bubbling.
Tongue tip on the wooden spoon says it's done.
Somehow we all sit down to dinner,
touch hands as we reach for bread.

How to Pack a Bug-Out Kit

Mother made the greatest apple pie
on Earth. Father showed me how
to bait a hook, sharpen a knife on a stone
and how to bleed a radiator so the hiss
settles into our cold bones like a fog.
In the trunk of my car I keep a wool blanket,
bottle of water, the lighter I took from Chris
at a Suicidal Tendencies concert in 1985,
and some stray hairs that could be my daughter's
or maybe the service tech who inspected
the car last month. He said the tires are good
for another 10,000 miles, but the brakes
won't make it through winter. $400
gets me back on the road. Fall is coming.
I already feel the chlorophyll retreating
from the street maples, animals burrowing
as deep as they can get. I'll pack a shovel too,
remember the apple pie, light on the river
where I camped with my father and brother
when the fire's hot coals burned long
after we'd fallen asleep. How smoothly
our knife cut through rope. When even
the cicadas' songs slipped into dream.

Addendum to the Note for
John Keats' Grave Marker

"Here lies One Whose Name was writ in Water."

All evening, sitting around the small fire,
we looked up and talked about Venus,
how much she stood out among the stars,
how the night looked blacker, even
the pine trees behind us leaning south
from decades of hill wind. And as smoke
rose above our heads, my daughter, her friend
and myself, our small worries in the small world,
chatted a little about the antics of flames
far from the troubles of others, cocooned
in our openness like survivors on a life raft
while the big ship is sinking.
Later that night another beacon
shot across the sky, the Space Station, three men
from different countries looking down
on the little swirls of water around the earth,
our names written in its rising and falling.
All of us pressed together by gravity,
everything blending into everything else,
disappearing with distance, the one thing
we can count on, but don't want to.

Marigold

It's crazy how easily some things grow,
like these marigold seeds scattered
three days ago and already green wings
like emerging mayflies sprout from the tops
of flower pots. Tulips, on the other hand
are more plant-and-pray, those regal
heads sometimes reluctant to rise from
this clay soil, and because poetry
does this to people, it's tempting to give in
to signs, to read every sunshower
or blight as a conversation with tea leaves
in a carnival mystic's tent. Let's not do this
today, with half the people on the streets
covering their faces, others daring illness
to strike them down. Some things grow
virally, spread the way rumor does
inside a church. Others need extra light,
a catalyst timed to tell a dormant vine
to wander. I tell my anxious daughter
to breathe slowly through the cloth, that not
all breath comes easily, how we need
to sit down in the cool morning and talk ourselves
patiently into the world. Even these flowers
must ready themselves for summer,
the sun trying to make things right.

Planting Strawberries

Maybe I waited too long, or not long enough,
to put the small wilted plants in the garden,
but that's what hope does, twists your arm
just a little, pushes you through the door. Outside
the sun slips below pine trees where crows
gather for an evening service, such terrible singing
I haven't heard since my kids, now grown,
gleefully tortured Handel in the school auditorium.
I watched the teacher's face as she led them
to the stands, shushed them until the music started,
then all at once their voices opened, flowers aching
toward the audience, each following some imaginary
sun across some future horizon, my daughters
with them, mingled in the world's chlorophyll,
the sugar in them turning into small, beautiful fruit.

How to Camouflage

It's a matter of becoming the music
in someone's head so they have
to look through you. In a park
pigeons land on the still man
and take food from his hands,
not knowing they've become more
than pigeons in the process.
In the forest just try to tell one
straight pine from the next,
each planted after the timber company
left and sold the ruined land.
That nuthatch knows, and marks
the best bark for another day.
If you stand in tall grass
long enough, ticks will find you,
make a home of your dark places.
Be nothing to the trees, ignore
the pollen filling your lungs
or gnats gathering in the tracks
of your tears. Underneath your feet
fungal strands are growing stronger,
carrying messages from root to root
only the aspens really understand.
One spore can change the whole forest
the way one lie repeated becomes gospel.

The Glaciers

An hour's hike into the gorge
through mountain laurel and hemlock,
July's heat steaming off each leaf blade
until I reach brooks no one bothered
to name, water tumbling like otters
through boulders the last glacier broke
before retreating into history.

Only small trout here, palm-sized
mountain jewels trying to survive,
and I'm crawling on my knees to meet them,
toss a fly I tied in winter into a riffle the sun
hasn't reached since Thursday. What day
is today? My daughters are far off
in cities. My wife is working at home
 online. My parents are aging
in the usual way. Bees labor
among the knee-high goldenrod.

Sometimes I understand why
there are gods and why
we drag the dead with us
through our lives.
Let all this. Every moment
its own untouched forever.
Somewhere glaciers still move
at their slow pace of elsewhere.
The beautiful and crumbling world
happening at once.

Sunflower

It's not even large as sunflowers
go, and the leaves droop with beetles,
but it's been a long summer, and to wake
finally in August to a flower the size
of a pie plate rising like a lamp post
over the garden seems a reward.
Across the street the neighbor's
flowers stretch toward morning
like they're looking down the driveway,
but he was carried out with a sheet
pulled over his face last spring.
Now his children empty the house
bit by bit every weekend.
At night deer and groundhogs
ravage my tomatoes and beans
but the squash vines sprouted
from winter dinner leftovers reach
from mulch pit to the neighbor's
house with no sign of stopping.
It's easy to leap from garden
to metaphor, like crossing
a bridge from one small town
to the next. It's not a choice
over what happens. You plant
and watch things grow. You drive
and get where the road takes you.
Sometimes you wake to rain,
and sometimes yellow petals
still damp with dew on a humid
morning can mean everything,
no matter what everything means.

Half Crumbled Silo in a Half Fallow Field

Say there's enough ruin to go around.
Say the song the bats keep to themselves
is a song of longing, calling out
to the night's open palm when the difference
between a palm and fist is what you know
about words. Like *ruin*—the kind covered
by decades or weeds, a word that changes meaning
when the land changes hands. The news today
says kids are breaking. What they know
is the ground is shaking underneath them
and believe that's all the future holds.
Not the answer to the bat's night song.
Not the way grain in an old silo
will sprout or mold depending on the whims
of weather or whether this abandoned farm
means someone picked up and moved, or
curled up and died alone like the cryptids
only fanatics truly believe.
We can't move on. The world's smaller
than a palm now. It's only when evening
over this forgotten place starts seeping
up from the ground and cloaking every color,
every sound hidden by another,
that for an hour you can't tell
the birds from the bats
but for their song.

How to Select a Survival Knife

It's not the steel or the sharpness
of it—any rough flint can make a fine

line of an edge. It's the care you take
separating skin from muscle, lifting wood

from other wood to carve a spoon, a stake,
a cane to walk you home along rip rap.

It's the jobs you've lost, the furnace finally
beaten into silence in February, every car

that let you down in the morning,
the maps that failed to get you home.

It's what you depend on when the difference
between sharp and dull is a full belly.

It's not about the shape the blade holds
in the sheath or folded against itself

in your pocket, it's the shape it makes
in your hand, the shape your hand makes

holding it, how two hands form a prayer
when you lift it above your head.

When You're in the Middle of It

I've stopped trying to scare the deer
away from the garden. September
tomatoes still ripen on the vines.
Two fawns, skinny as clouds, look
into my porchlight at night, trip
over each other as the mother
flicks her white flag in caution.

Months and moonlight cover
the same yard as usual, same
world as last year, though my wife
coughs and recovers in the upstairs
dark. Every night there's more
of them. Standing under the pines
like broken wind chimes in a storm.

They want what I want, what we all
want. For each season to do its best
and move on. For life to be easier
to live. I took the fence down today,
spread the best fruit out on the lawn.
All I can do as the days get shorter,
the cold we knew was coming, come.

Blessings of a Dog

"You must praise the mutilated world."
—Adam Zagajewski

She chases the threadbare tennis ball
across the kitchen, dives under a chair, slides
to catch it mid-roll then trots back
bearing the wet gift in her mouth
and asks with her eyes and paws
for me to throw it again. And I do,
again and again repeat this simple joy,
until tired she throws herself onto my lap
and gnaws my knuckles. Sometimes I want
this forever. The way a perfect fall morning
lingers in the scent of walnut trees.
All the grief of a summer we carried
like water, spilling with each labored step.
She's still a pup, has enough play in her
for twelve years or so. I know how that goes.
You love, they love. Everything goes on
like it should until it doesn't. She doesn't
know there's something broken in the world
that a ball can't fix, like a bearing that makes
the machine run smoother. Like the smell
of woodsmoke in the air that reminds
us of childhood innocence, even though
something in the distance is burning.

What We Make of the Mountain

They're bringing martens back
to the Alleghenies, and drilling wells
to light the cities, and did you
know that salamanders caught
between your fingers, can shed
their tails and live, one wriggly
bit still sticky in your hand
like a kiss, the body already
gone into leaf litter, and even
though my cousin sold his land
for a summer home in Florida,
the voles kept scratching tunnels
in the ground, tiny eyeless
guerrillas of young suburbs.
When the casino broke
turf for irrigation, they found
mastodons, tigers, bones
that make the coelacanth
look young, and yes, the sea
once rocked here, and buffalo
nursed their calves, but we've
got black mold in the resort's
new dining room, ragweed
in the AC, customers
demanding attention.

Objects in Mirror are Closer than They Appear

as is joy, sometimes, or grief, growing larger
in the back of your mind like an unopened letter
shaking in your hand, a knock in the engine
you know means trouble. Life, too, quietly
everywhere, whole constellations of it thriving
on your eyelashes, between the dandruff of your scalp
like deer in the woods you don't know are watching.
Maybe you see a truck in the mirror, growing larger,
faster than expected, a lump in your throat
or growing in your breast. A storm on the Doppler
radar, darkness over the house. Don't think
about the baby sea turtles you saw on TV—
how each flipper step toward the sea
was a triumph over hawks, gulls, destiny,
even the rising sun an enemy against the refuge
of waves. Every sunrise a revelation.
Every sunset a relief. Every few minutes
your small car shudders with the backdraft
of a tractor trailer carrying frozen chicken or copper tubing,
passing the crumbled blur of another accident
at 90 miles per hour. The moon swooning
into the rear-view mirror lifting oceans,
moving metric tons of plastic into the mouths of whales,
the tilt of the earth shrugging off axis.
How we get used to living at this speed.

Nightscape

Tonight's snow falls
like moth wings
spiraling after they burn
against a hot lantern,
and that brings to mind
the chronic disquiet of winter,
how landscape covered
in fractaled ice seems
to step outside of time.
I watch from my kitchen at 3am,
while my neighbor's light
also winks on across the yard
and I wonder what
old or new anxieties
keep him up too.
From the bent pines
between our houses,
lit only from windowglow,
two deer stumble
through drifts and disappear.
And now the snow comes
faster, the world getting older
and desolated by cold,
everything getting heavier
with the work of bearing it up.

II.

Legacy

For no good reason I'm thinking
of my grandparents as I lurch
up this hill past lean-tos used
by through-hikers among
second and third growth timber.
So many things they carried—
the Swedish church songs
from Wisconsin, the cemetery
in Mount Union that marks
an older pandemic. My home
is full of their artifacts: steamer trunk
from Malmo, the wedding walnut
dresser, old saws the shipbuilder
used in the boatyards of Brooklyn.
I used one to cut through boards
for garden boxes, steel teeth
still sharp as ice. It's fragile,
this kind of memory,
like the forest I hike through,
each tree reusing the legacy
of the fallen, nourishment
from decay. Every year fewer
of the old ways survive
to reseed the land. And I can't
help but wonder what my own
children will carry of me
from one temporary shelter
to the next.

Weeping Willow

When you're eight years old
and pull enough of the whip-like
branches into your hands, take
a running start and lift your legs,
half the tree may bend, but still
you're flying for a little while,
swinging in the sun's arc
over the rock your brother calls
the Volkswagen because it's almost
as big as the neighbors' blue Beetle,
and when you let go, wild leaping
out over the rock onto soft ground,
rolling down the hill into the always
wet part of the yard, you know that
sting in your hands from landing
will go away, just like everything,
the last two times your parents packed
to move, some new tree waiting
at the new house, your knee bruised
again through your hand-me-down jeans.

How to Start a Fire in the Wind

You have to put your body into it,
cup the flame like an infant
cups a breast because it can fill you,
shed some light into the shadows—
maybe winter started early and stretched
into spring, maybe the jays that settled
into the spruce forest are thinner
than last year because your dreams last
only as far as you can see in the dark.

And damn that wind anyway. What business
has it lifting shingles from the roof
only to scatter them in the field?
I challenge it to a duel. Its persistent
muscle against my need for heat. Love,
let's talk about love. This dark
has nothing I can't wish away
with the weight of my body
cupping a single match, blowing
oxygen into the kindling until
all the world is ablaze.

Pheasant Court

It's been years since I thought about
the ring-necked pheasants that came down
from the woods and into my yard
when I was a boy. My mother
woke me one Christmas morning
to tell me they were here, their heads
and necks shimmering like tree tinsel,
their long tail feathers bright
as new copper pipes. They waltzed
among our frost-covered garden,
dipping and strutting over the furrows,
then disappeared at first sight
of our young collie Caesar.
My father said the game warden
stocked the woods for hunters
and sometimes strays survived
nested in the trees near the dying farmer's
fields. His children sold the land
for housing tracts, named new roads
after the grace that passes so quickly
in and out of our lives.

Box Turtles

My father had to stop me
when the collection reached eight,
and he found me walking a road at night,
flashlight scouting the shoulder for more.
I can't truthfully say if it was reverence
or envy for the way they carried
their burdens everywhere. I was only ten
or eleven, knew I liked how slowly
they walked, easy to catch, trusting
in the sureness of their shells,
how even wild they'd open up quickly,
explore the pen I built for them in the yard,
and soon enough they'd take berries
directly from my hands.
How can you not love an animal
whose body is hinged and hardened
against the world, but will stop
in the middle of a road
to stretch out its neck, testing
how many cars will pass overhead.

How to Track Animals in the Woods

Imagine a deer or rabbit
standing crossways to the sun.
It keeps its head in shadow
to cut the glare, its legs bent
to run or leap like morning light
on Baptism Creek. Imagine next
how it leans forward to eat, chews
with its eyes closed against gnats,
ears angled to the turns air makes
through rhododendron caves, aspens
quickening in the breeze. And then
imagine yourself older still
than luck or health should carry you.
Both dreams live in the same
sunlight. Hope is everywhere
and danger and sickness too,
and sometimes clouds darken
the trail and sometimes the moon
still shows itself in the middle
of the day. The deer, its hooves
supplicating into soft earth
is still listening up ahead.

Sycamore

Higher than our house,
one foot in a crook, another
perched on a branch, but barely,
the whole tree swayed in a good wind
while sixty feet below my mother
shouted things it's lucky I couldn't hear
to get me down, but from such heights
I could see clear to Parker Street,
the old stone house where Darin
lived until his father hung himself,
and then the shopping center
and the woods that rose behind it
like a storm cloud, something
worth knowing moving inside it,
something you could know
a little about by watching
from the tops of trees
like an equal.

Sycamore II

Some of the oldest trees
in these parts, seed pods
big as goat balls.
They shed their skin
in patches like iguanas,
and the old ones,   that sentinel
tree along the dark part
of the Bushkill,   they split
their trunks into caves
big enough for a child to hide.
My grandfather showed me
one along the Delaware
older than the Constitution,
and when I squeezed inside,
heard the buzzing of bees
above my head.   I thought
it was voices, all the small
animals that hid out fire
one time or another,
history whispering
its needs from the wood,
and when I close my eyes
and think of him,   crooked
as a branch, I still hear
their warnings in my head.

Lesson

It was my grandfather, *Poppy*, who taught
me shame when I broke the garden statue
while playing ball in the yard. Shame was
all the old mid-western Swede said, shaking
his head as he tried to find the broken pieces
of a ceramic angel among his stiff and orderly
rose bushes. And I stood there, thinking
shame over and over in time to my arms
swinging like useless clock weights.
Shame the way he didn't scold me
or make me sit indoors all afternoon.
Instead I rode my bike around the block,
searched the old shed for something to play.
Shame the way I went to bed, unpunished,
his voice a shadow on the bedroom walls.
But mostly I remember when I found him
later, bent over a table with glue, glasses
slipping down his nose as he fit the pieces
back together, that he patted the open bench
beside him, showed me how to make things right.

Mayapple

Like memory, even landscapes
are unreliable. One day this hollow
between two ridges reveals nothing
but frost and the snakish bloodroot
groveling between fresh breaks
in the forest mulch. Today a sea
of mayapple tumbles like river
rapids into Six Penny Creek.
It was narrow once, fast-flowing
until winter opened something
upstream that water reclaimed.
In his last year my grandfather
showed me the mayapple's
granny green bulbs hidden
in the plant's parasoling canopy,
a faerie's forest only ten inches
off the ground. The whole
tumble of them connected
by rhizome trailways, roots
joining each to each, a family
sharing what it can before
all is lost to the next season,
building something that could
last the weather.

How to Use Knots in the Wild

One end goes around the lodge-pole pine,
one through the loop, two half hitches
secure the ridgepole, three bind the devil.
A bowline can get you down a cliff face,
but a sheepshank won't last the day.
Stop a fraying cord with a snake whip
or burn the edges as a last resort.
What if you need to cross a creek?
What if the wind feels different
since you've been alone, like
the weight of leaves shouting
against your back? You need
to tie things down, keep the world's
hungry jaws away from what
little you've got left. You probably
left a faucet running, a burner
on the kitchen stove. Something
you forgot to say when you were
younger. Trust a clove hitch
for your guy line, a timber
for your pack. Faith goes on
without you. Regret follows
you home. Tie your tent poles tight.
Snug your food in a tree.
Get across that creek tonight.

Confession

It's true my father came to find me
standing nearly in tears in a cornfield
one October when I was 9 or 10, fresh
tracks of the combine still soft
and the bony stalks broken into angles
like rows of skeletons resting
with their knees pointed at the moon.
The night before, the corn still stood
tall, and older boys filled their sacks
for Mischief Night before the farmer
harvested it all for winter feed.
I missed it, stuck doing homework and chores.
Father didn't approve of tick-tacking
neighbors with hard-fisted corn,
but he believed in a son's need
to roam in the dark with friends,
to feel the cool night without parents
watching, and so he crossed the small woods
between our house and the farm, helped
me pick through the battlefield of scraps,
deer watching quizzically from the field edge,
until I had enough to launch a siege
on every picture window in town.
We lurched our ammunition back home
in silence, tearing our pants on barbed wire,
and me swearing to myself I'd never tell a soul
how my father helped a lonely kid
make mischief, how he carried half the load.

Watching a Flying Squirrel

It doesn't really fly, just falls
better than the rest of us,
a calculated leap across empty space
from oak to pine to maple.
Life is risk, and love too. Between
one safe branch and the next
uncertain one lies hard ground
or rocks. When my daughters
were born my wife and I imagined
branch after branch for years within reach,
not the ones we fell short
or that left us hanging by a claw.
Now we talk about the years
we spent on the ground, wondering
how to get back to a place
where everywhere we looked
we saw trees.

The Dark Part

Sometimes I miss the clank of bottles
left by the milkman on the front step
or the way a gas station payphone
in its small glass coffin might ring
in the middle of the day. Maybe
it's the long coat my mother wore
when she walked us to the bus stop
for school, and the oil can my father
kept in the shed for bike chains or tools.
Now I return to the smell of apples
cooking in a pot after the whole family
spent an afternoon in trees, dropping
them so our little sister could pick
them off the ground. The strange words
our grandmother used for things,
and boxes of ration kits she saved
from the war years. The civil defense
helmet I wore to play in the yard,
basements lined with jars, Candy cigarettes
at the corner store, and the dark part
of the attic with hat boxes of yellowing
photos, how stern the men looked facing
the camera as if that moment was the close
of a play, the curtain on its way down.

Happy As

In high school my friends and I would drive around
in Stem's van, high as kites, we'd play a game
called *Happy As* and name three things
we were as happy as, like apple pie,
skipping school, making out with so-and-so,
then try to beat each other with joy
until the weed buzz wore off. One friend
shipped to Kuwait after graduation, then Afghanistan
in the first wave, and never came back.
Another dropped out of college for rehab.
The third I bumped into ten years ago
with not much to say. Me bald. He'd gone gray.
Worry and doubt, those close companions of age
worn across our faces like tattoos.
Other troubles roam around in blood cells
for years until they find something inside you
to break. Joys too, but never by themselves.
I wanted to ask him what he's happy as,
if he could name three things, and I'd try to top
his list with mine. Happy as the bills paid on time.
Happy as a call from the kids. Happy as the resting
heartbeat that's been wrong about so much.

III.

Talking With Birds

It whistles. I whistle back.
Dactyl, dactyl, spondee, followed
by a third or fourth bird hidden
in the forest's miraculous meter
and I am almost sure this choir
singing behind my tent is not
random. Pole-straight hemlocks
and red maples hold back the sun,
tower like saints of memory. I'm alone
among old bark tattooed with lichens,
so at ease with what the world wants
of them they die standing up.

As the trunks reach skyward
their lower branches weaken each year
and fall off, useless in the dim
below the canopy like the duff
plumage of young birds as they learn
to fly. Some of those birds
are telling me about the uses of wind.
How when they catch it right
it can carry them anywhere,
maybe across the river gorge
where more birds are turning
every hour into music, reaching
for the wind, asking it to hold them.

Fireline Trail

This trail, marked in yellow blazes
for the mapless or lost, where lookouts
once kept eyes awake for smoke and lightning,
begins in white pines, the edges
needlesoft and quiet, then blends
into proud old chestnut oaks standing
straight a hundred feet in a kind
of wisdom. At the top, where paper birch
lean toward the gorge, unwrapping
in the almost noonness of the sun,
a meadow filled with low blueberry
bushes stretches until the mountain
bends to the river. I pick my fill
of ripe ones, miles from highway
traffic and the river now dying
from mine acid. Here, so much
free sweetness within easy reach,
the world must be playing a trick.
Maybe it's not that life is hard. Just
our expectations too high. *Eyes bigger
than your stomach*, my mother used to warn.
I'll leave most of the berries here.
Begin the switchback down to the car,
back through those oaks, the quiet-dark
of pines, the day haze that leads
toward home, the taste of blueberries,
the whole marvelous mountain,
still on my lips.

How To Build an Emergency Shelter

There are ten ways the body crumbles:
injury, sun poison, hypothermia,
hunger, loneliness, arthritis, the howling
of coyotes in the distance, rain soaking
through your clothes, memories, especially
memories. The taste of Sunday morning
blueberry pancakes on your grandmother's
everyday dishes. How you wept when
the sugar bowl broke. How you weep
when the sun goes down on another
absence, and part of you with it.
You could surround yourself with debris,
boughs from the forest floor. Ferns
and their deer ticks thirsty for you.
Or lean against a rock, pressed
into the cold cheek of the world
to ride out the night, hope morning
warms up the cliff face, hope
evening restores what was broken
and sleep spells escape. Nothing
you can build from the gatherings
around you can keep the world
out. The secret, as always, is to place
one thing on top of another, the way
we pile earth over the dead
to cover our losses.

Cottonwoods

Walking under winter cottonwoods
I think how diameter and height
are poor ways to measure a tree
or anything for that matter. What
about the black scar of lightning
on the mossless side of this one,
or how a small village of mushrooms
argues over a rotten stump? My father
is about as tall as me, but scarred
from scalpel and the bird tracks
of stitches that sewed his heart
back in place. If these trees talked
perhaps they'd gossip about moss
and recall that winter all the flickers
disappeared. When I visit my parents
now, we share meals, talk about
the empty house across the street.
We make vague plans that could be
next week or the next century.
Time is only good for so much.
Like the body, it's warmed
by memory. When no one near
is looking I lean into the oldest
trees, press my ear against the parts
that look like they've lived through
the hardest weather, and listen
for that silence I pray is there,
the sound a heart makes between
each old worry, the sound we want
most but are still afraid of.

Bird by Bird

In time the milfoil
will thicken this lake
so that even beavers
can't navigate its old
darkness.

In time water will
crumble the stone bridge
that joins the new
forest with the last
old growth timber.

If not for dreaming
hellbenders would
still be spawning
in the cold slack
of the Allegheny.

It's the slow changes
not the sudden ones
that wear us down,
that spot you've been
watching on your skin—

the way a country falls
bird by bird until
one spring you notice
the heavy trees you loved
are so quiet.

How to Tell if the Water is Safe

Don't ask the leopard frog about
the osprey in the sky. Don't ask
the stickleback about the pickerel
stalking in the weeds. Cryptosporidium
is tasteless. Hope isn't. It swells
the tongue, shrinks the stomach
into a surgeon's knot with both
loose ends dragging in your throat.
If you can count the number of dead
fish along the bank. If you can hear
the buzzing of larva stagnating
in a green pool. If you can stand it
enough, like waiting in line in the wind
to vote for another dream killer,
like paying toward a debt
so large your children will inherit
its weight, paying for so long
no one remembers where it began
or if it ever gave anyone any pleasure.
Only then should you cup your hands
and drink.

Perseid

Summer's promised meteors finally appear
when a Pennsylvania sky gets too dark to see
the bats. Parades and picnics are over.
Now the season feeds on itself until thin.
Last night my neighbor told the same joke
he told me last week about a lawnmower,
a man slumped over the handle crying:
must be going through a rough patch
he says. The punchline hanging in the air
between us like fireflies flinching from
the weeping willow. And even though I know
this light show overhead has been traveling
the same path for eons, I laughed.
It's only debris burning itself finally out.
Some lights are brighter than others
though dimmed by distance. I ask myself,
who do you miss? I stopped counting
when clouds moved in to divide our small
world from the eternity we're still learning
more about every day. We expect these lights
to return, though it takes a rough year to arrive.
That's what it means to be a human today—
gaping in the dark, watching the brightest stars
blow themselves out.

Baptism Creek

I've camped in these woods
for years and never seen a bobcat,
though the forest service says they're here.
Today I hike down Well's Hill, cross
Baptism Creek where it murmurs up
from an old wound in the Earth
then dodges boulders and beech trees
to enter Trespass Pond, a water named
for mystery as much as Baptism.
In November every sound becomes the crunch
of leaves, the rising and falling rhetoric
of chipmunks stockpiling their dens.
Remember when we counted off
the safe days since we breathed without
fear? Families avoiding each other
for months? We know it's out there,
another threat waiting for us to drop our guard,
our hunger for others' touch sometimes
unbearable. Yesterday rain kept me
in the cabin. Today sun but cold
follows me down Baptism Creek.
I don't need to see a bobcat to believe
one is out there in this forest.
Its feet padded for stealth. Its nose
and ears tuned to warn when I'm coming.

Gunpowder Homestead

Consider what centuries do to forests—
a kind of strengthening of the muscles,
a thickening of bones, but old homes—
they crumble stone by ported stone.
And ghosts may come and go
like hummingbirds in the afternoon,
strumming through glassless windows,
lingering under arches where someone
passed daily in and out of shelter.
It was probably hard here, coaxing
a life among sharp edges, winter air
thin as Bible pages. Each spring
the creek rose to take half
the valley, and each summer sedges
shrank to seeps only worms
could live off. Now, a hundred
and a half years later, some reason
for what they made here, for breaking
oneself against the land until it breaks.
And a rightness too, for what remains—
four crumbling walls, the hearth where
fires hushed winter back, now
retreat into hellfetter's tangle,
ruins on the one hand,
succession on the other.

One Mountain Seen Through the Trees of Another Mountain

Maps never show a view like this,
yellow blazes on trees leading
to a ridge, the trail so close
to the edge just walking feels
like falling. A five-day trip away
from towns or news of the world
brings me to moments so sublime
I forget myself. Anthropologists say
joy in landscapes is burned into our DNA,
distance a factor of dreams. Below,
the lake is starting to ice over, a cold
that's been building for years. And this
mountain loop I'm walking could go
on too. In the next county there's a hill
called Hope, and here one called
Sanctuary. I'm walking down it now
to a lake the settlers used to feed
their families. Its feeder creek
powered the old iron forge also
called Hope. So many things named
for what we want. Or is it what
we have? My legs grow sore
on the rocky trails I climb
to get home. This path called
Daybreak might be the one.

The Way Back

After hiking the horseshoe loop,
I build a campfire, pour a tin cup
of wine, then coffee,
listen to rain on the cabin roof
and think about how
there are so many points
where things could go one way
or another. I could have followed
the blue-blaze trail, reached the ridge
before sundown or taken the lower trail
by the lake following the crazy duck calls
and hunters coughing in their blinds.

Hours later rain has snuffed the fire
and I'm halfway to being two-thirds
drunk. Sometimes going back
is tougher than going forward.
Regret a hard cousin to inertia
the way brothers will keep moving
apart once one stops talking
and another takes that for an answer.
I think how birds' thin bones
can hold onto the whole sky,
the world just a small trembling thing
shrinking beneath them.

How to Apply First Aid in the Wild

Trouble the wound to heal itself. Trouble
the earth, the river, this starry night bleeding
with animal eyes. Trouble the trees to not shed
their leaves before fall, to fall only from age
and not the tractor, chain, and backhoe.
Trouble time to smooth over scars, for scars
to act as warnings, and warnings to sing.
Sing to suppress pain. Sing to embrace it.
Sing to ease the trouble out of old bones.
Trouble the song to lead the wanderer home.

Another Name for the Moon

Tonight another moon named
for rage or hunger or a legacy of want
strode across Cabin Road—
a drama old as dreaming,
but every year I stand under it still
with my mother's Lutheran loyalty
to Sunday's seasonal anthems.
And as I stare at the ancient guide
grown into the ritual of its myth,
I think of the people in my house,
shifting slightly as they sweep through
their dreams, almost mouthing
something, the way my mother's
mother talked about her phantom leg.
She called it a gift waiting in heaven.
Said she knew it was always there,
even if out of reach.

IV.

Fallout Shelter

The brochure reads like a luxury magazine
for the tactically-minded: bomb-proof
reinforced steel door, two-foot concrete
walls, HEPA ventilation, granite
countertops and floors.
And you can stock the pantry
with canned goods pre-selected
for shelf life, nutrition, something sweet
for the one-year anniversary
of the end. But today, rains poisoned
by history or greed feed
my vegetable garden. Weeds
fill the cracks in my driveway.
I've enough coffee and bread
for the weekend. The kids will phone-in
status reports of their lives. My 401(k) looks
like a heartbeat, but at least it's beating.
In a month I'll pickle cucumbers, store
them away for fall like a prepper
with a short attention span for hope.
You can add security cameras,
motion sensors to alert you when
the wandering hordes of half-survivors
come banging. You can electrify
the door, compost your shit,
finally finish *War and Peace.*
Wait out almost any trouble
you can afford.

How to Signal for Help

Where there's smoke...
there's just another person
burning up their dreams in the night.
It's all around us now,
brushfires everywhere so
much it's hard to tell
one epiphany from a cry
for shelter. Better to move
to higher ground, mind which
way the wind is blowing
and where the floodwaters lap
at the hospital's closed doors.
Help isn't coming. It's always
been here, standing next to you
like a stranger.

Last Mint

Even at the dry hinge that closes
summer into fall, when the mower
cuts down the last surviving mint,
its bright scent lingers
like a spiderweb after rain
the way some lives do, thriving
even when all signs say otherwise.
This mother of bees through summer,
accent to tea and gin, is even
now preparing roots for winter
as our transitory geese announce
their night flights, leaving us
behind a season's dead weight
before long evenings with firelight.
Still, a fresh green shoot
is trying to hold out
alongside red rose haw
and pumpkin creeping
along the ground, something
new to wrap your hand around.

Epistemology I

When sunlight through trees
catches spiderwebs,
it travels that fine thread
like dew, slides
with the wind
from one branch
to the next.
It's December
and cold this morning.
I'm thinking of my father
alone in the hospital
and wonder if the web builder
ever knew what a sight
it was making,
so much like breathing
or music it is,
rising and falling
the way notes follow
each other without knowing
how they fit together.

All Birds are Good

All birds are a kind of good, especially ducks
running like toddlers across the lake surface
before take-off, and the way a hen will turn
to watch the slowest of her ducklings
try to keep up among the pickerel weed.
And in the red maples, gray catbirds
shriek at every wind-wavering limb because
they don't want to disappear into the evening.
Pigeons, of course, the way they strut
like bellhops for breadcrumbs, but when
sunlight catches them—iridescent
as the bowls of oyster shells.
Owls we all know are good, watching the world age
like grandparents or the kind neighbor who smiles
when you give her some fresh tomatoes.
Let's not forget the buzzard, who pees
daily on its own body to cleanse itself of lice
after it worships what others leave behind.
But let's not stop at birds. Frogs too
are a magical good. Especially tree frogs
when they chorus with cicadas in the willows
on hot July nights because both know how hard
it is to turn from one thing into another.
Also mice and skunks. The little brown spider
who crawled across my book tonight.
The earwigs in my garage.
The steampunk centipedes that inch up
the basement stairs in winter looking for sugar
on the kitchen counter. So much is good
I can hardly stand it. Also poems, all poems
no matter how bad, are good because like ducks
or earwigs, they go vulnerable into a world
that forgets what good is. Let's call it all good
because anything else is defeat.
The small things we step on and break.

Sounds that seem to haunt the night.
Ordinary meals, the flat pillows
that do their best to cradle our tired heads.
The pain we avoid talking about.
Absence. Heartache. What the world
teaches us every day. Because even that proves
there's a heart when some days
we're so, so close to losing it.

To the Climate Activists Who Threw Soup at Van Gogh's Sunflowers

On the one hand, yes, it's destructive,
but what can you do when
there's so little left to ruin?

If we knew the great fires and rising seas
were coming, would it make any difference
to the river of cars on highway 80?

But of course we did know,
and the ships kept unloading goods
by the millions, and plastic rafts

collided with plastic rafts until
they formed a new continent,
and forests made way

for warehouses until the sun traveled
all day without resting on raw earth.
And sometimes we complained

about the weather and sometimes
the weather complained back with floods.
But if anything, humans are good

at getting used to bad situations,
and the future was always
in the future, so why not

match ruin for ruin, one bright
flower with the wither of another.
Let's strip the sunlight

off a masterpiece,
if we're determined to live
in the dark anyway.

Epistemology II

I hardly remember what
if felt like to sit mornings
or evenings in the backyard,
scanning the trees, the sun
working over the grass. Me not
sneaking glances at my phone
or laptop, not grimacing at what
the far-off world was ruining or
who said what to whom and when,
and just be satisfied, at least
for a little while, with how far
my eyes could see, the scent
of whatever blooming or rotting
around the yard, a dog pressed
against my leg, not worrying
about how long this will last.

Epistemology VI

The thing about geese
landing in the baseball field
on a September morning
is the thing about tadpoles
in the shallows of Baptism
Creek is the thing about
a ten-foot sunflower
bending again toward
sunset is the thing about
waiting for news alone
late into the night
and what night
promises and what
it promises is morning
and what morning promises
is whatever you're able
to muster the daily
revolutions of light
to dark say about
hope or need and that's
the thing about the
heart which is the thing
about everything

How to Find Your Way Home from Anywhere

You got here on your own, after all.
And yes it's dark, and yes, there's something
shuffling in the trees out of sight,
but isn't there always? Maybe
a predator circling your camp, waiting
for some spark in the fire to turn your head
away. Or maybe it's those years
of bitterness that broke you, finally
catching up, or the fatty foods
building up a dam in your arteries,
or something you inherited from your mother's
mother that splits old memories
in unpredictable ways, the way sparks
will flare into flame without warning.

You're closer to the trail than you think,
just one wrong turn away from a diner
with a *Free Wi-Fi* sign hanging in the window.
But instead you sit here, staring into the trees
waiting for something to happen, waiting
for morning, for rescue, for someone
to make things right.

Planting Pawpaws

Their seeds look like coat buttons smeared
in the fallen fruit's ripe custard.
Pushing four of them into compost pots
in fall for planting is a category of defiance,
a confidence that seasons and shadows,
sunlight when it comes, will be kind,
that life will limb into sturdy bones,
that bones will leaf and bloom, and blooms
expand to fruit settlers here called
Hillbilly Banana, or Quaker Delight.
A complicated sweetness that surprises
in a season when everything else is dying.
My therapist friend says you can talk yourself
into hope, a new life, but it's work
to force something bright from a dark place,
to search the woods for a fruit tree
that bends between borders and wastelands.
A neighbor gave me a bucket of them,
and I spoon the pulp, seeds and all,
directly into my mouth, smooth
the small stones with my tongue and spit
them into my palm. Some may rot
in the planter, may be scavenged
by squirrels or broken by ice in winter,
but if I'm lucky, if all the promises nature makes
with fingers crossed and eyebrows furrowed,
then one day I'll lift ripe pawpaws
off the ground and give you some.

Have you reckon'd a thousand acres much?
　　—Walt Whitman

Today from a ridgetop I can see a thousand
acres ripened with maples and chestnut oak.

The last road an hour out of sight. Rain
a season old still draining from spring cricks.

Is this what we save the soul for? Losing
grip on a cliff edge, a river still remembers

what it was like to carry coal dust,
the occasional body, over white rapids.

Still a million raptors navigate the pass
every year, chasing summer into hollows

and gorging on sparrows. Four sharptails
just now cartwheeled in the wind. A bridge

is falling somewhere. There are protests
in Tehran and Prague and my father

with a wire navigating his heart. I'm tired
of walking today, but the sky is blue-

crayon blue, and the ridgetop haired
by low blueberry bushes stained russet

by October, so I'll settle for a solo moment
of meditation while fewer birds migrate

south again, some music in the wind I can't
put a name to, stuck in my head like hunger.

Epistemology III

Seasons are not merely abstractions
on a calendar or the ritual
we make annually to drive from one
resting spot to another. They're more
like metaphors, carrying the weight
we give them, the way this day
in October feels both like the orange
glow of turning maple leaves
and the church of acorns on the trail
already beginning to decay. Death
everywhere, and life, and all the places
in between where sunlight rests
for a moment, and also the places
it doesn't. I step over old logs slowly
becoming soil, a colony of mushrooms
kneading its fingers into pulpwood
gone soft from years of rain and snow,
sun and wind and rain again. Because
watching is measuring, and measuring
wants to be understanding, and sometimes,
when I sit long enough watching ospreys
roll over the lake or see the new work
of beavers downing trees for winter's
threat, I believe that maybe I do.

Taking Down the Lights

Every celebration has to end,
lest we get too easy with joy.
Because a length of twinkling
bulbs around the house
can't change that cold rain
turns to ice, and even small
lights take energy, draw something
out of us until we've had enough.

So foot by foot I pull the wires off
the eaves, drop the strings onto
salted sidewalk and frozen grass.
Boxwoods freed of their stars
let winter just be winter, not
a soft gloss we gaze at for a while,
a story we made up from childhood.

Each year feeds into the next
like small rivers flowing into
larger ones. Days of joy. Days
of not. Eddies that swirl for a while
then disappear. You've lost people.
I've lost people. We take the lights
into our hands, pack them away
until the darkness calls them back
again, when we've almost gotten
used to living without them.

Epistemology VII

Maybe because the endless boredom of the world
is a reflection of its anger, or exhaustion its

closest companion, how too much of this or that
heartbreaking or headbreaking or everythingelsebreaking

of the days—there are still days, sometimes more
than you deserve, when the sunfish gold of forsythia

blankets the neighborhoods you drive through,
or the fiddleheads rising from their dormant husks

like any religion's savior might do, force a downshift
in the body, when music sounds redemptive again,

and food feels restorative again and even the waters
you stand in fishing, not perfect or pure, and probably haunted

by mine acid or farm runoff or just beaten down
by centuries of apathy, that you notice the snapping turtle

slowly existing near you, and the eagle, yes, really
a bald fucking eagle, just existing above you,

and what else could you need but this moment alone
in the vibrancy of April, how the best possible meaning

is no meaning at all—sun's slight angle crawling
through the wild dogwoods, pale mayflies dipping

their egg-laden tails back into the water,
the beautiful stubborn boredom of life.

After

When you've thanked the rescue party,
drunk all the clean water you could hold,
and peeled the tired boots off your blisters.
When you've looked back at the mountain
and the nights shivering against the cold
bark of a dead tree. When you've eaten
surrounded by other people, watched closely
how their mouths form words like your mouth
as they lift and hold the utensils of normalcy.
That's when you open to gratitude,
to the emergence from darkness
that comes after, that holds regret
and forgiveness in the same hand.
But still, all this fresh comfort and return
to life reminds you that losing your way
is easier than finding it back is a lesson
you will learn more than once.

New Year's Eve Poem

The snow takes its meaning
from what's under the snow.
Our footprints from the people
who made them and where
they're going or have been.
The ruin of the mill, a few stones
still stacked by the forgotten,
takes its meaning from the creek
tumbling below it, some fish
too, cold in the current. The wind
from the things that move in the wind.
My family standing with me
on an old bridge that connects
the hiking path to the paved road.
Snow on both sides of the bridge.
One kind of remorse to a new
unexplored territory. One kind of weather
and another we try to prepare for.

ACKNOWLEDGMENTS

I am grateful to the editors of the journals, magazines, websites and anthologies who published poems from this book, some in slightly different forms or under different titles.

Adirondack Review: "After Survival"

Atticus Review: "Sunflower"

Bear Review: "Baptism Creek," "How to Tell if the Water is Safe," "What We Make of the Mountain"

Bracken: "Cottonwood"

Cider Press Review: "Confession"

Cimarron Review: "How to Signal for Help"

Cutleaf Review: "Pheasant Court," "One Mountain Seen Through the Trees of Another Mountain," "Last Mint," "*Have you reckon'd a thousand acres much?*"

Cultural Daily: "Happy As," "Planting Pawpaws"

Literary Field Guide to Northern Appalachia: "Mayapple"

Native Fruit: Poetry and Fine Art Inspired by the Pawpaw: "Planting Pawpaw"

Freshwater Review: "Epistemology III," "How to Camouflage"

Ginkgo International Ecopoetry Prize Anthology 2023: "NASA Announces Plans for a Peopled Mission to Mars"

January Magazine: "Box Turtle," "The Way Back"

Kenyon Review: "How to Apply First Aid in the Wild," "How to Use Knots in the Wild"

Lake Effect: "Taking Down the Lights"

Laurel Review: "The Glaciers," "How to Build an Emergency Shelter"

Louisiana Literature: "How to Pack a Bug-Out Kit," "Proper Use of a Survival Knife"

Nimrod: "Life List"

New Verse News: "Making Tomato Sauce with my Daughters"

One Art: "Fireline Trail," "Weeping Willow"

Pine Hills Review: "Addendum to the Note on John Keats' Grave Marker"

River Heron Review: "Planting Strawberries After Work"

River and South Review: "Nightscape"

Sand Hill Review: "Marigold"

Sixth Finch: "To the Climate Activists Who Threw Soup at Van Gogh's Sunflowers"

Schuylkill Valley Journal: "Bird by Bird"

Southern Poetry Review: "How to Find Your Way Home"

Tar River Poetry: "Watching a Flying Squirrel"

UCity Review: "Blessings of a Dog," "When You're in the Middle of It"

Valparaiso Poetry Review: "How to Talk with Birds"

Verse Daily Poem Prize Winner 2023: "Blessings of a Dog"

Whale Road Review: "Gunpowder Homestead"

* * *

I'm grateful to the many people whose contributions helped in the writing of this book including Brian Beatty, who saw nearly every one of these poems in early draft stages; Hayden Saunier, Amy Small-McKinney, Tom Mollouk, Susan Charkes, Liz Chang, Joanne Leva, Sean Webb, Doris Ferleger, and Chad Frame my long-time writers' group and friends; and Jack Bedell, Todd Davis, and Ethel Rackin for their thoughtful comments on this manuscript; and especially my family for going along with it all. I'm also grateful to the Pennsylvania Department of Conservation and Natural Resources' Bureau of State Parks in whose cabins many of these poems were written.

I also wish to extend sincere thanks to everyone at Cornerstone Press for their hard work and thoughtful attention, including editor Brett Hill, cover designer and media director Samantha Bjork, the sales team of Sophie McPherson, Madison Schultz, and Autumn Vine, and especially publisher Dr. Ross Tangedal.

GRANT CLAUSER is the author of several books including *Muddy Dragon on the Road to Heaven* (2020), *Reckless Constellations* (2018, winner of the Cider Press Review Book Award), *The Magician's Handbook* (2017), *Necessary Myths* (2013, winner of the Dogfish Head Poetry Prize), and *The Trouble with Rivers* (2012). His poems have appeared in *The American Poetry Review, Kenyon Review, Greensboro Review, Tar River Poetry,* and anthologies including *Ghost Fishing* and *The Literary Field Guide to Northern Appalachia.* His poem "Blessings of a Dog" won the 2023 *Verse Daily* Poem Prize. He received his MFA from Bowling Green State University where he was a Richard Devine Fellow. He teaches in Rosemont College's MFA program and is also a senior editor at *The New York Times/Wirecutter.*